"It was evil and I loved it."

— St. Augustine

SEX WITH GOD

Sex With God

Revised edition — expanded to include a new
Book II, *The Ashes of Eden*

Poetry copyright 1994 by Thomas O'Neil

Illustrations copyright 1994 by Ty Wilson

First edition of *Sex With God* was published
in 1989 by Indulgence Press

"A Letter to the Boys in the 24th Century" appeared
originally in *Christopher Street*, Issue 109.

Library of Congress Catalog Number: 93-61845

ISBN Number: 0-9622398-1-X

WEXFORD PRESS
185 Claremont Ave., Suite 6A
New York, N.Y. 10027

CONTENTS

— Amen —

BOOK TWO: *THE ASHES OF EDEN*

To the memory of Brian Mangum,

once my other, unorthodox religion

SEX WITH GOD

By Thomas O'Neil

Illustrations by Ty Wilson

SEX WITH WHOM?

Of all the sad aspects of being gay, there is none so disheartening as that smug religious notion that heaven is a straights-only club.

Homo-hating straights wouldn't be so smug about it if they didn't have the Bible behind them. The so-called Good Book makes a good half dozen references to homosexuality that are not only disapproving (Leviticus 18:22, the classic citation), they are outright assassinations (we are "worthy of death" if you ask St. Paul and the author of Leviticus 20:13). Worse, once snuffed out, we're told that we'll never get past the Pearly Gates (1 Corinthians 9-10). We are invariably left wondering: What the hell is hell going to be like? Will Lucifer turn out to be a drag queen — call him Lucy — whose idea of eternal bliss is plucking out our eyebrows while singing Sophie Tucker songs?

With one exception, all Christian churches today condemn homosexuality thanks to stubborn, literal interpretations of those scriptural passages. The United Church of Christ is the only mainstream faith that formally allows the ordination of gay clergy; all others damn us to hell in their official doctrines despite what the occasional gay-tolerant minister or priest might preach when he strays in his sermons on a charitable Sunday. As a result, God the Father and Mother Church invariably play star roles in the lives of gay people of sincere faith whenever they dare to fall in love. Throughout Brian's and my romance, we felt their hovering presence all the time, and usually just on the other side of the bedroom door, huffing and hissing about what those two boys might be up to in there. Their meddling, in fact, began just as our, and this, story begins here, on the eve of Brian's and my first meeting, when I finally broke out of the Midwest at the age of 25 and fled east, all the while deciding that, if the Bible's right and I'll never see heaven, then I might as well go searching for what salvation I could find in being gay.

I arrived in New York City at Christmastime, 1979, to behold Babylon at its most bedazzling. Every year Manhattan dresses up like a gaudy whore to celebrate the virgin birth. Back then she represented to me a great fag hag who time and again had proven herself the most Christianlike proponent of the Yuletide spirit by gathering lost gay souls to her bosom at all times of the year. I would soon learn that she had room for one more as I approached her — drawn by the sparkle of her holiday jewels bursting with gold, red, and green — while on a private quest to find love and a career in publishing. In short, I came to New York to be a writer and a married one.

Suddenly unshackled by Midwest and Catholic prudery, I struck out hellbent through the city's gay singles scene — "the bars, the bookstores, the bonhomie" — wherein I had hoped to discover a promised land.

Then, eureka.

One Wednesday night in early December,

1983, while stopping by the only gay bar on Manhattan's upper, upper west side — a now-vanished hellhole called the Knight Deposit that was surrounded by noisy Latino bodegas and snake-eyed crack dealers who roam the sidewalks at 106th Street and Amsterdam Avenue — I found Brian. He was a 25-year-old office temp (read "actor" by night), who was also bona-fide forbidden fruit — black, Protestant, an ex-Marine, gorgeous — and I was white, then 29 and unemployed (a "freelance writer" when introduced at cocktail parties). We quickly became a work of theater all our own as we surrendered our passionate natures to a whirlwind of dating diversions: horror movies, runs through Riverside Park, midnight rides on the Staten Island Ferry (just 25 cents roundtrip — we were broke in those days), bacchanalian evenings at piano bars and cabarets (on expense account, because I was then on a magazine assignment to explore them all), and cheap pasta dinner parties (so we could show each other off to friends). In time, we got around to doing all the other things that other couples do — we had spats, split up, made up and finally moved in with each other (that old story). Come morning after those early blissful nights together, and in between failed attempts to write novels and plays, I would rise at dawn to pen those freelance magazine assignments whenever I was lucky enough to have them, while Brian dashed off to temp jobs or acting auditions. Ultimately having to decide between the corporate and theater worlds, Brian chose the corporate one when he was offered a starring role at a top bank where he had been answering the phones as a temp. He didn't have a college degree, but he still must have given a commanding performance on the job because, within three years, he was promoted to vice-president and given a paneled office overlooking Wall Street. That's how winning he was.

Our friends were just as carefree, delirious, and desperate for love as we were in those days. There was Andy (my flamboyant childhood friend who moved to New York soon after I did and, excited at the find of so many tempting fruits around him, moved into the bathhouses and there sucked the sour apple of AIDS) and Crazy Ed (a frumpy, sweet-natured librarian and sometimes caterer who desperately wanted to be loved but ended up having a fatal affair with drugs). Soon after I learned that Brian and I were living doomed lives together, I discovered that they were also fated. Just a few months before Brian died of AIDS, Andy and Ed died, too.

Being a budding writer, I was bursting to write this drama down as I lived it, but each time I penned another poem, I kept having to deal with the intrusion of the disapproving Parents. If this writing seems too ferocious here and there in its jabs at the church (yours, mine, nearly all, by the way) and God, it is not necessarily my fault. They were allowed to intrude on my private world of poetry, just like they haunted me in the world they created, only after they accepted one condition. While writing, I announced ahead of time, I would apply Newton's Law: every action would have a corresponding reaction of equal force. If I suddenly felt an undeserved pang of guilt or shame, I decided to give the divine Duo a body slam of equal oomph right back. Fair's fair and those are the rules, I figured, even when sparring with the Almighty. In the early 1980s when I wrote much of this book, the religious right was just then declaring its latest holy war against gays. The New York tabloids were filled almost daily with

Cardinal John J. O'Connor's tirades against fags, delivered with old-style fire and fury from the lofty pulpit at St. Patrick's Cathedral. Down in the nearby City of Brotherly Love, where children apparently deserve to die of leukemia and the homeless from exposure, Philadelphia Cardinal John Krol actually told a reporter, "The spread of AIDS is an act of vengeance against the sin of homosexuality."

Such religious blasphemy is hardly new. St. Thomas Aquinas once argued that homosexuality was evil because it seemed "unnatural" to him in those dark ages before the birth of biology and anthropology. Today, however, we know better, hallelujah, thanks to studies conducted by the likes of Indiana Professor Paul Gebhard, who has reported that homosexuality exists in all animal species except those that are hostile during the mating season. In addition, recent breakthroughs in genetic research have finally substantiated that the sexual inclination is inborn. The reality about being gay, therefore, is not only different — and quite opposite — from what my church and others say, but every Cardinal in the Holy See and, for that matter, every bug-eyed, fag-bashing televangelist ought to rush right off to confession to repent past preachings as soon as they figure out the following: being gay — imagine this — is a gift from God.

You would never know it from what the Bible has to say, though. Enlightened theologians argue that the scriptural condemnations of homosexuality as an "abomination" should be taken as seriously today as the Bible's similar denunciations (and using the same term "abomination" in Old Hebrew, interestingly) of people who eat pork and mix two different kinds of cloth, but few religious leaders have ever seen the logic of that. Everyone needs someone to hate — even love-thy-neighbor, church-happy hypocrites, apparently — and gays got the job long, long ago. Jesus Christ never denounced same-sex love in the Gospels, but most of His churches do today because of other sections of the Bible written by men or women who never met Jesus or a burning bush and probably weren't even speaking officially on the Divine's behalf. At least the author of one scriptural chapter, 2 Corinthians, had the courage to say he or she was not God's mouthpiece in chapter 11, verse 17: "That which I speak, I speak it not after the Lord." Which leads us to wonder: Why is the author of Leviticus infallible?

When I wrote the first edition of *Sex With God*, I dared to shout my angst to heaven over this religious humbug as I meantime boasted of the sudden salvation I found in my new love for Brian. I soon got my comeuppance for messing with the Almighty. A few months after the book was published, we learned that Brian had AIDS and I began penning Book II — *The Ashes of Eden* — in which my angst became volcanic anger as I wrote about the slaughter of the innocents now descending on our house. No one was more innocent, or a better example of true Christian spirit, than Brian. Long before he knew he was infected with HIV, he raised money in the AIDS walk-a-thons and donated long hours as a GMHC buddy who graciously took on patients who weren't even gay when other buddies refused the assignments. He ended up specializing in straight, mean drug addicts, who would spew all their farewell rage against the world at him personally as he did their laundry cheerfully, prepared their food with a warm smile and emptied their bedpans.

Aside from my own selfish rantings on religion, this combined volume should be read as a love story, although a bittersweet one since faggots are damned in the end and God always wins. But enjoy it, dear reader, feel the passions that we once did and join me and my departed lover's loving family in missing one Brian Mangum, who died at the age of 34 on April 8, 1992 at Cabrini Hospice in New York City. How ironic, in the end, that I should have lost him in a Catholic hospital. But it was a coincidence, I assure you, that occurred only because his doctor just happened to be affiliated with the facility.

It was there under the brooding crucifixes and bloody oil paintings of the Sacred Heart that my Protestant love at last slipped away from me and dropped to Dante's Seventh Circle. I am deeply and honestly grateful to everyone at Cabrini who tended to him in such a genuinely Christian way near the end, but I must share this thought that terrorized me at the time and, I hope, be forgiven for it today.

There we were finally at the entry to Hell and we discovered that nuns were the gatekeepers.

New York City
April, 1994

A post script to the reader: This book's illustrations are the record of a witness to this story — Ty Wilson — a longtime friend, who not only became familiar with these poems as I wrote them, he was often, I'm afraid, unfairly subjected to them at the time. Usually it was at Brian's and my Pennsylvania cabin on one of those let's-get-out-of-New-York weekends when, noting the presence of a captive audience, I couldn't resist interrupting Ty's pensive musings on a dancing fireplace with a sudden, aria-styled recitation of my latest tirade against Christendom. He has obviously forgiven me since then just based on the quality of his artwork here. The illustrations are so good, in fact, that I am tempted to think they must be divinely inspired. How else could he know so intimately the soaring feelings that Brian and I once considered ours alone? The exhilaration of our falling in love? The terror of the night sweats?

He knew the latter in part because he was one the few friends who volunteered for the ordeal of bedside hand-holding once Brian was confined at home or in the hospital. So he was no mere witness to this story, come to think of it ... no, he was part of it. And for his part in it — especially the hard part — I'll be forever obliged. Ty, by the way, is one of those rare proofs in life that good things do happen to good people. Over the many happy years of our knowing him, Brian and I had the ultimate pleasure of watching our once-struggling-artist pal rocket to star heights. Perhaps there is a God.

SEX WITH GOD

SEX WITH GOD

OK, Lord, let's settle this.
This sort of thing doesn't
make John Paul Two very happy
and if mom and dad knew, they'd be mad as hell.
So how come if everything we have
is a gift from You,
that one whopper was nonrefundable?

I used to want to give it back
that shiny package that arrived one day
shortly before Your gift of whiskers,
the pretty box done up in silky pink ribbons
and scarlet (O'Hara) wrapping,
the one that makes the boys
who play basketball hate you.
And what a hilarious surprise
there was inside—Jesus!—when
a Judy Garland puppet popped out of it,
dressed up in drag,
like a Rock Hudson doing Barbara Stanwyck.
(What a sense of humor.)
But I like it OK now, Lord.
It's sweet and insane
like a mouthful of moon cheese.

Thank you.

There is nothing in the world
like talking
sex with God.   8/13/84

1

— Appointment in New York —

He's here somewhere
between the ferns
looking doe-eyed
and clutching a Lite beer
like a walking stick.
Some Sunday morning, once we're married,
he'll nearly scorch
the blackberry muffins
while waiting for a commercial
that will never come
during "Mass for Shut-Ins."
But it's impossible
to recognize him in this lineup
tonight along the bogus brick walls
at these s(tand)-and-s(tare) bars.
He is blinking
nervously behind the smoke,
a queasy bride-to-be.

You, in your older brother's blazer,
will you be the one I savor
someday as sweet as the honeydew?
The over-eager cherub
who sits on the lip of the pool
table was last week's conquest,
but he'll never surrender
the wildlife
and, in fact, I remember,
preferred snapcrackleandpop.
I like the one in the Wall

Street uniform best,
over near the stack
of Lite empties near the men's
room door, but he's staring at someone else,
actually the cherub, who is preoccupied
calculating how much to overtip
the pretty bartender
in order to make
his peasant omelette.

Dear Jesus, hear this prayer:
deliver me
from this place of the frightened
statues and false affections
night after night
to, say, the honeymoon suite
of the St. Francis
Hotel with the one You intend to be my salvation.
We'll order up a lite breakfast
of doughy treats on a tray
sprayed with baby's breath
and don purple ties before strolling out to High Mass
at the cathedral where we'll exchange
a whispered vow in the back row
and wash ourselves clean
in the blood of the Lamb.

But for now, there,
along the wall,
let the moving finger
reveal him so I can move on.

                              2/17/87

7

Jesus Is Seen at a Gay Bar

I caught
sight of Him that night,
looking sexy in His sackcloth
and ridiculous in a Groucho Marx disguise,
there in the corner behind the *David* statue,
listening intently to the angel-faced
tramp who knows how to dish with the best of 'em.
Too bad Madonna
was belting out "Papa Don't Preach"
so damned
loud we couldn't overhear them.
The tramp actually looked like he was
putting the moves on the Almightly One,
but Jesus just played it cool
while He chatted over His glass of Perrier
later seen, magically,
to be filled with an amusing, off-year Medoc.

"What the hell
does He want from us?"
some queen
snarled that night over his pinot noir.
"Christ, we're not exactly the choirboys
of the Holy Seraphim having their Christmas party.
And, by the way, Jesus, we got St. Paul's letter,
again, just the other day: addressed
to the insolent slanderers who exchange
the Truth of God for a lie, deserve death,
and must forfeit the Kingdom.
There was no return address."

But it was a night to remember.
Jesus joined us in a few choruses
of "Over the Rainbow" around the jukebox
and disappeared before Last Call.
He left His keys on the bar.

2/11/87

A LETTER TO THE BOYS IN THE 24TH CENTURY

There's no way for you to know
the excitement that the return of the Black Death caused,
a 14th-century celebrity on the evening news
autographing personalized Certificates of Death
for little boys
who could never own
their own marriage certificates.

He'd wave to the cameras
like the new heavyweight champ
as he planted poison blossoms
along Cherry Grove, made the steam
of the bathhouses rise as sweet
as Buchenwald's; and gay
became sorrowful; and love
became death and families
forgot the same sons
they once lavished
with graduation parties,
aspirin and catcher's mitts.

He had a fan club, too,
and danced at the discos
without scaring the Screen Set.
Because he came to the AIDS of ridding
perversion from the population,
ministers and mothers especially loved him.
Last heard from, he was thinking
of running for Governor of Georgia.
It was a Second Coming hailed

by the faithful everywhere, you should know,
like Babe Ruth
come home to pinch-hit for the Yankees.

But there are some questions
I have for you in the 24th century:
How do they like their Mr. Death now,
blueeyed boys?
Have they named a chain
of successful health clubs after him?
Did he win in Georgia?
Is his profile on the penny?
Are you there?

1/8/87

MASS CONFUSION

An item in *The New York Post*
reports God was mugged
last Saturday night—
by the Cardinal of the Archdiocese.

He gave his Boss
a good rap on the noggin, too,
when he snuffed out
the candles at a Chelsea Church
and slammed shut the tabernacle door
on the Body of Christ.
Seems the man who wears
the most expensive gowns in town
wants to fortify the gates of Heaven
against those fems who exchange the Sign of Peace
on 16th Street.

Mass may now be offered
again in catacombs, they say;
next week's paper will tell.

A message for Your Eminence:
the giftshop at St. Patrick's
Cathedral is a little overpriced.
Pardon this bargain-hunter's heresy,
but I'm a mite perplexed
that you've given a home
to the moneychangers in the temple
while evicting
penitents praying for grace.   3/5/87

How did they ever do it? I've always wondered —
Saints Anselm, Aeldred and Paulinus —
slip past St. Peter at the pearly gates
hiding their deflowered bums
prissily under wings
pulled down.

That homos have a place in Heaven
must mortify the Pope,
who should look into the lives of the Popes.

The great Michelangelo isn't listed, though.
No doubt it was the mortal sin
he must have committed
in his mind each time his hand
moved   up   *David*'s   thigh
and
he
dropped
his
chisel in awe.
Surely, he could have bought
his friend the Pope's indulgence at any time,
but spent his commissions on wine
instead sipping it in the piazza
while thinking of Tommaso
and the love that the artist
said draws
one up   heavenward.

8/11/87

15

TALKIN' DIRTY

These are the routines
if you're a queen:

Go out on a pier
and the leatherboys
bite you in the tit
and slap your bare ass, sneering:
oh yeah what big balls goddamn

Struggling actors in between auditions
blow you in the back row
of smutty movie theaters:
oh oh I'm gonna cum shhhh!

Interior designers
invite you back to their place:
oh silly me did I forget
to give you a tour of the bedroom darling?

Other guys don't care,
do it anywhere,
and rarely say anything to each other.

Rome may say it's all a sin,
but sometimes even a most pious monsignor
playing God in his private sacristy
has been known to tell an altar boy
defrocking after Mass:
blessed is he who cums in the name of the lord

7/31/87

16

To Young Men Who Have Felt the Same Longing

Let it go,
the sadness
of being gay
and the fear of inevitable
rejection some nights
in a crowded bar full
of boys who don't look
any better than you.

The bathhouses, the bookstores,
the bonhomie
might just be a rendezvous
with sexual satisfaction,
but we accept it and safely so,
because it's all we've got.

That, and the hope
that Richard Gere
might be gay
and call someday.

2/1/87

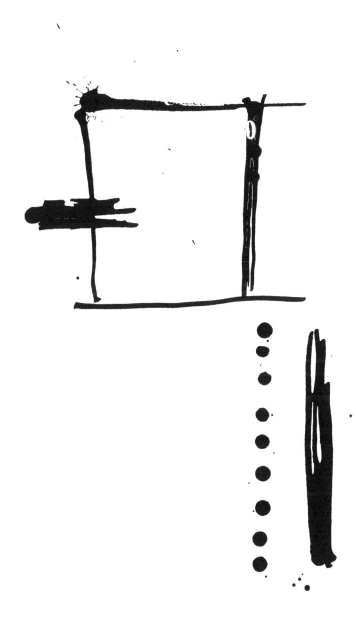

The Brian Poems
— and —
Other Intercourses

BLACKBIRD

Blackbird,
the vast shadow you cast
when you descended on my life
was midnight cool

We met when I cast you a madman's gaze
wild with drink
and you took me home
to play Lena to calm a stormy soul
and it worked
and we wrote the evening off
only to meet again when you
called out
coldly in a crowded bar
on a January night
to freeze
and I did
and we met steam giants walking that next morning

We got hitched so quick
it was almost as if we had to
and knew a whirlwind honeymoon
of hallelujah singing in the shower,
wild scatterings of your pet pigeons
in the park as we'd jog,
and confessions in the dark hours
of insane family secrets
and a future date with Oscar or Tony or Emmy
(you were going to be America's Ebony Olivier,
remember, and I was a wannabe Williams).

In those days it was just the theater
of everything that mattered most
— as long as we got to the mad scene.
In the mornings, though, you would soar off
to Broadway auditions too soon
leaving me behind, my urges aching,
left alone to finish an overdue magazine article
on investing in microchips
across the sea
in Ireland

A few days later you'd finally return:
One time I let the buzzer scream at midnight
as I watched from a high window
my blackbird panic at an unopening door
below; kept locked
because of a lover's spat
and there was another boy's body
downstage between the sheets
that night I ultimately shipped him home
and returned to our nest alone

Loved one,
why do we fight like this
as 30 comes closer
a dead ringer to the face
of the frightened (not so) nelly (really)
who thinks his grave winks at him
from the hot end of a cigarette?

We went to the park one night,
tired as always,
and the flare of fireworks overhead
signalled a disaster at sea below:
the blackbird saw the true madness finally,

not realizing it is an S.O.S. really
crying out for a sexual port of storm.

Blackbird, blackbird
your curtain opens again
on a distant stage tonight
and I have this small prayer
waiting for God:
let his lines be remembered.

Herewith,
an open letter to all the other happy boys:
the sheets I've spoiled
have ginger on them.
I
am the perfect
lover's love.
I have the trophy
of men who still call
remembering a passion
they carry with them
like syphillis in the soul.

And though I'd much prefer
to make waves with another, I have come
to this conclusion: I'll rejoin
the madcap regatta sometimes
when I can sail out insane on a summer's night
and while the blackbird is chasing Olivier's hem,
but I must bail out
during intermission
like a hooker who suddenly finds her heart.
But that's cheating, isn't it?
And I cheat so well at cards.
I sometimes think I see the world best

knee deep from a sixpack,
but someone may never grasp the theater of it.
It's not Lear in a storm anymore.
But of the world that I came to conquer,
I am winning, winning, winning.
My lover and I are staying a rocky course for now,
the telephone brings news
of new assignments every day,
and my prose sings back to me strongly
sometimes
like a blackbird

Blackbird,
your pigeons were in the park this morning.
I walked by the river
greeting dawn 'round the tree trunks
when they came
looking for stale bread for young chirpers.
I told them you were away, at another theater,
playing a madman

7/21/84

27

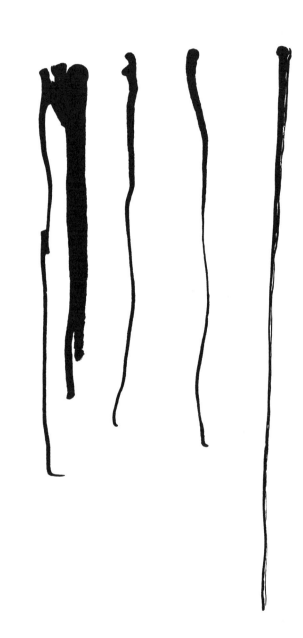

A Sexual Apology to My Father

The same brooding Jesus
you once hung on my bedroom
wall made me this way.

But, oh, how I would have loved
to have extended your line,
to have held that gilded mirror
up to you, history's prize
for having given the gift of birth.
You would have seen your tiny face, dad,
giggling once again under a Christmas tree,
slobbering on the wrapper
of a candy cane, and saying
things like, "Wawayouhaha."
His little pecker would have drawn
the same line so far into the future
we'd have lost sight of it
over the cemetery hill

where someday, you know,
we will be a family again.

But I fell in love
with peckers, dad.

A boy came to our door one day
when you weren't home
peddling a sachel full of escape,
the alternative lifestyle.
I bought the lot.

I sampled countless others after that,
in the fast lanes of Indy
and the fern bars of New York
at night, while I pursued
another immortality, for us, by day.
Some found me; others
I went shopping for.
But you'll be happy
to know, dad, I've decided
on only one, a chocolate bar
so sweet you'd want to bite
your own son-in-law
if you met him. Promise.
And mom would want to overdress
him in a scarf
of Hershey's foil.

You must know I'm going to win,
because I will outlive you,
and talk to your sisters
over your brooding remains
at the funeral home where
we'll swap recipes
and put a final period on your lifeline.
He was a funny man, my father, I will say,
but there will be no last laugh.

1/30/87

LETTER TO A FRIEND LOST TO DISTANCE

(TO ANDY)

You bastard, you left me
alone
with the battle against New York,
the braying of the evangelical crazies
in the subways — Yes, the end of the world
may be about to happen here, but I no longer
have the catty answer to give
those tired old queens braying
over their fruity drinks:
come on, why not, tart,
one last bang?

Home to hide under your mother's skirts,
a fleeing back to the womb,
to our hometown,
a Mistake-on-the-Lake with big fields
and little minds, the same
we couldn't wait to flee
after waking up one morning
and touching a wet dream.

In high school out there
we acted out *Becket*
to the wrong, catty crowd.
I, their class president,
even got pelted in the tit
with a paper clip.
In New York

we finally fought back
and acted our own way,
going our own way,
firing off barbs
at any old audience we'd choose.
Sometimes we were so good
we'd win an Oscar.

God, it was a dream
down Christopher Street
having you here
to ogle the leather-shop windows with
or to peep through the doors of our fairy bars
to see who might have dropped by that night.
Bette Davis or Miss Hepburn?
Oh, if only Judy Garland could see
how she looks to these Dorothys
dyeing to be her.

In those days
we swapped insults and wardrobes in Brooklyn
and beheld the true Great Kate on Broadway
together; and celebrated our birthdays alone,
braying against the insanity
and injustice of this place,
usually over a frozen margarita.
Our little joke was that you
were really Mrs. Tom O'Neil
and another one that ended with
"I'm going to kill myself."

You used to doctor me
and I wrote our shopping lists.
Alternately, we were each other's uncanny psychiatrist.
In (albeit outer) New York City

I gave you a home and a mail key.
I still have not forgotten
our lines
or the money you cost me in Brooklyn, "baby."
But all is forgiven,
if not forgotten.

Because we were sisters in Oz.
By the sunken skating rink
of Rockefeller Center I told
the first friend I really knew well
that I was gay. We laughed it off and carried on.
Oh, how we used to carry on.

When I moved to Manhattan
Ma Bell and your med classes at Columbia
kept us together. We would hold on,
desperately, to the phone line till dawn,
still reaching for that therapeutic punchline
while we cackled
at ourselves or reruns of *The Mary Tyler Moore Show.*
Christ, we would have recorded
those conversations if we'd been Neil Simon
after another million.
In the next life, promise,
we're gonna make it in show biz, baby, if we choose.

I woke up this morning
and walked down St. Mark's Place in the Village past
the bathhouse we used to call, sacrilegiously,
Church, that unholy place
where you would fall to your knees
and hear the angels sing
whenever somebody dropped his towel.
What nightmare, I still wonder,

must have finally found you there?

But Dorothy at last got back to Kansas, eh?
How's the wheat crop?
Here in Oz
the gayla you must know, has gone on
without you.

I have taken a lover, baby,
but then you know that.
It was at a westside cabaret
one night before you fled that he sang to us
with a strange approval in his voice
of a friendship he still cannot understand.
His microphone even waved
a blessing over us out there
in the dark where you told me in a whisper
that you might need a real psychiatrist.
You looked tired and like you might
really want to kill yourself.
But I got you through that night, too,
with a few clever cracks and frozen margaritas
just like we'd gotten each other
through so many others
with a doting
that so many mistook as a lover's.

In a way, when you left,
it felt like a world ending.
It is crazy to say it
and a catty remark
that you will probably have an answer for,
but I came to this city to conquer it;
you left defeated.

2/1/87

35

DIE RUNNING

This is not practice for the Olympics;
rather, an endurance run
through the thicket of adverbs, a match
of muscle against the steep metaphor
and a simple knowing
of the thrill
of the downhill
        adjective.
How could I ever have thought
that writing was a spectator sport?
Blame a fleet-footed F. Scott for that.
Press on.
Stay in shape.
Do not look behind.
The only thing that matters
in this life is to
die running.

9/30/86

PERFECT BOY

(OR, THE SERMON ON SUTTON PLACE)

The host of the cocktail party
took immediate note of his impeccable clothes.
"You have an eye for fashion," he said.
"Thank you," said the boy, holding
his scotch-on-the-rocks smartly.
"It really helps if you know the rules:
The shoes match the belt,
the socks match the shirt."
"You're kidding, aren't you?" the host inquired.
"Of course," said the boy, lying coolly,
but then that was the perfect thing to say.

Perfect boy,
framed by the hors d'oeuvres table later,
you leaned over the brie to talk to me
like a monarch acknowledging a serf.
At expensive cocktail parties like this one
everyone smells like old clothes.
You smelled like Christian Dior, off the rack.
"I'm not going home with you tonight," you fumed,
eyes glaring like a furious papa.
"At your place you never change the sheets."

Outside, later on,
six scotches after half past nine,
in the little park that looks so much like Europe,
I have a craving for old cheese.
You sit silent, a mouthful of venom.

The black iron fence keeps neatly at bay
the promenade of old tuxedos and fur.
Still, they know.
Two boys out of bed still look like boys in love.
Our backs to the dark river,
we await the final battle.

"But the passion is gone!"
you spit the poison out, leaping
on a park bench of midnight green,
playing it like Lear mad
among the elements — feet kicking, arms flailing.
Your fist hits its target like a marksman who'd practised.
Ouch.
Your next attack is frontal:
"I know you've been cheating on me.
Damn you! Damn you!"
In a penthouse overhead,
two lights blink off;
a dowager swallows
her heart pill in the dark.

At the party
you gave a speech on artistic integrity.
Here in the park
you take a pee through the ironworks.
I cradle my smarting cheek like a lad with a toothache
while the occasional actor in you
finds his next line, disjointed:
"Just 'cause you got dimples,
you think you can say anything!"
Perfect boy, you took the wrinkle
out of that dimple all right.
My fashion plate has finally crack-
ed, become unraveled.

What must the police think
passing by —
a brown boy beating up a white boy
in Sutton Place
South?

But we do make the perfect couple, some say,
yet how little they really know
my heel-clicking marine
with his automatic smile
who could pass inspection in a mudslide
and his boozy fallen angel
who thinks he can turn vice into virtue.

How we argue sometimes
at night
when I undo the perfect corners of your bed
so I can stretch out and sleep the lumberjack's sleep,
and how we battle over bad Broadway plays
or turn a discussion over tableware
into trench warfare.
It pains you to the boot heels — doesn't it, my dear? —
that this love remains a secret
from the others that I love
while you wear it like a medal of honor.
Yes, how that can manage
to snuff the passion out.

Next come the tears
and the pathetic confessions
of lies and betrayals
even Christ couldn't forgive,
as the black river washes by,
our love history slipping south,
and the moonglow overhead

reveals a wrinkle in your collar.
We are not alone.
A couple covered in shadow nearby
makes a silent servant's exit
while the Greek urn in our Old World sanctuary
watches, stone faced, and seems to understand.

Perfect boy,
when you came into my life
on a Wednesday in December,
I became a man that night.
Here in the park
your pouting face
looks like you've finished a great journey.
I love you.
Come back.
Apologies are in order
for an imperfect Lord
who makes imperfect heroes.
Thank God, our little promised land,
New York, is a city
where New Years never ends.

Perfect boy,
it's late.
Let's go home.
I hate bad theater.
Under the bedclothes,
in our leg lock,
our bodies make a perfect fit.
Lights out, the vagaries
of color vanish
and our skins melt into
a cafe au lait so sweet
you could lose your taste for scotch.

I'll wait till morning
to tell you the truth
about what you really did last night:
your Bette Davis imitation
to a roomful of producers.
But you did it perfectly.

Tonight, I pledge,
a new journey begins.
Tonight, I promise,
we'll change the sheets.

1/3/86

PEEPING JESUS

It's the streetlight that still haunts me sometimes
remembering that
awful eye of God outside your window
never blinking
denying sleep to one of us
while you sailed off through dreams somewhere
remembering a ride on the Staten Island Ferry, say,
the night we shocked the subway conductor
by holding hands
and stood grandly at the railing
starboard side in a dark wind
and picked out the Statue of Liberty,
the two of us looking like Armenian immigrants
arriving in the City of Hope
with a fortune in chickens.

The streetlight, so stern,
knew even then, I think,
that boys who do with boys
finally get what God's eye's waiting for:
a portable purgatory for the asking
and a misery that visits you in dreams, too,
when good boys have to say goodbye.

Last night,
in a cabride up Broadway,
I picked out your streetlight among the many
as we sped past 104th Street
in a race against the meter.
It's still watching over you, I see

43

the light
sleep well

my little lollipop, my little babushka.
Goodbye.

8/21/84

WE ARE MARRIED

(OR, SETTING UP HOUSE)

Lover, it turned out cozy, after all,
spooning dinner every night from the same Farberware,
turning down one sheet
in our little room
while down below
the straightfolk come and go
looking for stray sons after dark.
Here we look for leftover ice cream
in the fridge — two queens on a homo's honeymoon —
having found something else
oh-so-delicious
for now.

The forfeit of privacy is the boon of one electric bill.
The mating of two album collections brings
the unexpected offspring of harmony
to the air of our castle keep where we throw
the windows open even in winter
and listen for the haunting
sounds of our own private opera
diva hidden and wailing behind a wall.
Here there is also only one last square
we must share at day's end,
where all arguments must be laid to rest
before sleep can come.

We adopt each other's eccentricities.
You drink Lite beer more and more;

I fold T-shirts before I put them in a drawer.
Just as we share the same secrets of the neighborhood:
a sale on champagne, the hot smells
from the bread shop, a smile
from the Korean couple who run
the new dry cleaners — so we take our blazers there.

But look how we behave like nations sometimes:
a pact on who waters the peace lily in the living room;
a treaty on TV; an armistice
over an air conditioner
left humming all night
so one of us can doze dreamily
for the drone of it.

Or like corporations:
lover, we have arrived
at a joint venture
in vacuuming.

Still, there are flashpoints
for potential arguments:
a jockeying for the shower,
a jealous guarding of the mail key.
But it's amazing — isn't it? — how soon
"bastard" becomes "darling"
when the freezer needs defrosting.

Up
here
in our
Harlem hacienda,
there are four running shoes under a bed.
We have found the long way home.
And here we also discover

a mutual love of garlic,
savor our red licorce and horror movies
and suddenly find an answer to:
"Where the hell did I put my wallet?"
The suspense can be fun.
A phone ringing can be for either one.
But marriage can't be as easy as this,
although up in Harlem we calculate
that one and one always equals one
no matter how we tally it,
such a miracle of modern math.
And there are other added surprises, too,
like a variation on the old joke
with the Jewish mother talking:
"Remember, my son, marry a man
and you will double your wardrobe."

But now the best part of all:
in bed, when the animal itch
cries out to be scratched,
we are there for each other
like practised masseurs.
Lover, I now know the curves of your body
so well, I could sculpt them from the heap
of your hot laundry I fetch from the dryer
in the basement.
It is why I fold the T-shirts so tenderly
upstairs.

This morning
the neighborhood bells of Riverside Church
celebrate a communion of sin,
a daily breaking of bread
for breakfast in a private sanctuary
that brings happiness to gays.

It is Sunday,
just before the tolling of twelve
when I see your spaniel eyes peep
over the bedsheet
and say
without the hidden lips ever speaking:
"Adopt me, darling,
but do not burn the toast."

9/10/86

A Tango in the Morning With Jesus

Let's consider the milkman for a moment.
What must he think when he arrives
with his burden of bottles
and the guilt of housewives had
and he peaks through the window for a Mrs. O'Neil
and sees us dancing between the cream-colored sofas?
Jesus, how You grip me around the middle, You cad.
Today we welcome in the daylight
through a latticed window
and step gaily on the cold carpet
celebrating dawn
in the broad, glorious sweeps
of a passionate tango.

Morning is such a curious salvation,
a new lease on life for two sweeps of the clock.
Let me put the tea on.
Will an old love call today?
Or the lottery officials?
I hope so.
I turn down the stove.
Extra cream today, Jesus?
Let's watch morning TV
and read Flannery O'Connor stories
to each other out loud
till the light wakes up the entire world
and You must vanish like a genie —
into a column of mist
like the tea kettle's —
and leave me so that today

a starving boy in Sudan
can happen in his path
upon a miracle of water and rice over a hill.

I love mornings,
new days,
a contract to repent and forget
the sins of last night.
Jesus, forgive me,
for these nights spent in the arms
of the other boy I love.
Your church in Rome has banished
us both to hell someday.
I love You anyway.
It's another new day.
Shall we dance?

1/8/86

51

INTERMISSION

Giving up theater, even temporarily,
must feel like a curtain falling
or a bad review,
but you've decided
that the show
of day-to-day suits at the bank job
and cash at the supermarket
must go on.

Your latest promotion
means you've been cast in a new lead role, dear:
break a leg.

2/3/87

My pin-striped banker
leads a checkered life at home
where his debits often include
a pair of shoes left discarded
in the main path of the living room;
the lazy 20-minute shower; a leg
left poking out between the sheets
as he sleeps; a shameless love affair
with the alarm clock snooze button.
Do the good ol' boys down
at the office know all this?
Come Wednesday morning he will ask
to borrow money till pay day.
Christ, some banker
he turned out to be.

But I imagine him at the office
looking cool as green money
while reading a report on third-quarter earnings.
Would that his bosses could only see us
on a weekend, though, reading
the Sunday *Times* together. The bully
in him keeps swiping the section I'm reading
because it looks more interesting
than the one he has. The paper rotates
six times before we finish it,
and the business section never actually gets read,
because at that point
we are usually too busy
getting down to business.   1/7/87

A Report Card for the Bully

For too long, buster,
you've ruled this playground.
We've played your games
by your rules
and you've always won.
It is time now
for your report card.

D, for conduct,
because even though you smile sweetly
at the principal sometimes,
you still look
like the schoolboy
who knows how
the-snake-in-the-teachers'-lounge
got there.

D, because you also
punch,tickleandbite.
Cheater! But I've
forgiven you.

Because of the time
you fetched me from the sweetbrier patch,
eyes bloodied,
and your fists took scratches on them.
You put me down on a downy bed
and we played a new game
of no rules and no losers
and very naughty.

I took my D, too,
for conduct, like a new man.

This week we'll have known
three years as playmates.
Our high marks in Attendance,EffortandPenmanship
have gotten us through another year,
unscratched.
I see, I fear
Graduation Day, buster,
far off,
but taunting us playfully,
beyond the monkey bars
and swings.

HOTHEADS

Heads bulging
with rage can spout
the most unsavory things,
even if nothing else
has gone wrong
but the pasta.

Lights out later,
two small heads about to spout
bulge under the bedclothes.
There is the feeding of a hungry mouth
in the dark, lips pinched back
to accept the prize
of a dark satisfaction learned
long ago and honed this moment
into artful love.
No one can tell
how the temperatures fall
when the blood still flows so hot.

5/20/86

BRIAN AT 4 A.M.

reaching for an exit in the dark
there is no interstate

pointing the way out
of the nightmare awake

shadows seen alone at this
hour against the bookcase wall
can scare the Dickens out of ya
and strand you broken down mapping
escapes in the ceiling plaster

when then like a runaway desperate
for a face full of wind
who cops a ride from a biker
he mounts himself onto my drowsing backside
in a fetal coil that brings him
home
and back
to the dream of our joint journey
slumbers too

8/27/87

A Bedtime Prayer to Save My Soul

Blessed be
the   fruit
of Thy womb, Jesus.

5/2/88

OREO

Black and white might make gray
to some eyes, darling,
but we both know
cafe au lait
is the way to be gay.

Because spice is the variety of life,
salt and pepper
dress up the fruit salad.

9/22/86

We are having a party.
We select the Ballet of the Chestnuts as a theme
so Julio can play the Borgia Pope.
The courtesans will bring
the chestnuts in sacks
that swing when their Calvin Kleins come off.
("He-he!" cries Julio. "He
who cums the most wins the silken tunic!")
("Makes a great smock!" cries MaryLouiseLouis.
"Oh! Orgy! Orgy!") But something is missing:
like a hundred cardinals coupling as in the good
ol' days of the famed Vatican bash and no nudes
slink against the floor to warm the chestnuts up.
I light the candelabra, winking
("Ready, boys! Go!") and await the rise
of cocks
like sunbursts.
We play hearts instead.
Fool Robert. He said a prayer
of thanks for the canapes.
Some party.

11/22/88

THE GIRLS ON THE BUS

leave their shopping bags
in the aisle
and badger a schoolboy
to make him
stand
up
on
command:
"Is this seat taken?"

They gossip
about a sale at Sak's
and kvetch in a confusion
of unfinished
stories of bridge
games, a nephew
who never calls,
their underwear
at a bargain and
garlic.

They can also
resemble a convention
of country doctors
sometimes, nodding feverishly
over a sister's lump
or her complaint
of mysterious pains.
Birdlike,
their heads

bob
up
and down
as the bus
dips
into another pothole,
spilling the schoolboy's books,
unnoticed.

When one of their stops comes,
so little a woman
can make a long goodbye
with her bags bumping through
two turns of the streetlight:
"Wait, busdriver! Wait!"

Alone
on the sidewalk
an icy breeze
catches her blue
standing
hair and the long walk
home with all those bags
makes her remember
sadly
how wonderful
it once was
being
a girl.

1/22/86

New York Traffic Jam

So many dreams
so big
on such a little island
heads collide

11/28/90

(Nether Garments) in a Nether Land

Two boys
(in their underwear)
sitting on a couch
touching knees
drinking coffee
hide
up
in
their
weekend retreat
in Pennsylvania.

Here,
the dull animalboys
of the garter and bra
have not seen us yet.

My love,
one Saturday
while I washed the windows
in the Poconos,
you flashed me through the glass
over the band of your
underwear)
and grinned like a schoolboy.
I grinned back with the same secret
of the)fruits(we'd just shared
before I turned to window-washing
that morning and you made the coffee.

Why is it
white cotton
(hugging) the (skin) (so close)
is so stimulating
to fruity boys, I wonder?
Perhaps it's because it was part
of the first (erotic) photos
we saw as boys
(in our underwear)
hiding
up
in
our bedrooms
at 14,
alone
with the J.C. Penney catalog?

A straight friend now tells me
he was fired from his job of 30 years
because his bosses
finally saw him in his underwear.
They hadn't.
But that's the bewildering straighttalk
of fellows
who do not savor
the same fruit of the loom.

5/19/86

LOST IN THE WOODS ON A SNOWY EVENING

(OR, THE PRISONER IN PARADISE SPOILED)

It is winterset
on a day the children have off from school
when He emerges between the petrified trees
looking like a lunatic-cum-saint.
Here at last, I think,
is the Bastard Boy of the Man
who confiscated Eden.
I want to ask Him a host
of things like why another god, by Jove,
lifted his boylove up to Olympus
on eagle's wings
while my Saviour points the winding way to Hell.
But He looks haggard and lost
and like He wants something
like a lift to Heaven
as He scrambles right then left, noticeably confused,
and late for a vision.
There, Jesus, between the fallen trunks —
I point the way out to Route 209,
but He ignores me
and heads only deeper into the wood,
following the bloodied path of a rifled deer.
"Happy Birthday!"
I shout after Him
on this Christmas Day
but there is only the cold silence
of finches under the snow
dying of pesticides.   8/24/87

69

A GALACTIC WONDERING ON WHY
IN THE WORLD YOU PUT UP WITH ME

A question, first of all:
why is it, love, that after nearly three years
of going where no man has really gone before,
you still haven't discovered the truth out yet?
That there's a Cling-on in your bed at night
who keeps the TV on and scatters
popcorn salt like burning stardust
between the sheets. He is watching
Star Trek reruns he knows too well,
still wonderstruck like an alien bride
at her first altar.
The familiar buzz of interplanetary battles
and the nova-bright glare of the primitive tube
keep your earthbound dreams at bay,
but still you lop a salt-studded arm
over the Cling-on now and then
as you reach for sleep in between commercials.
"I lovers you. Do you lovers me?" you ask,
invoking our private babyspeak —
genuinely loving, genuinely wondering —
as the digital clock nearby reports your office shower
now awaits you in six hours, 17 minutes
and counting, Captain.

The Cling-on plans to sleep till noon.

He gains five pounds
and you lose six,
doing situps.

He drinks too much from the altar cup;
you send back the wine.
He's allergic to laundry.
You gather two loads
in your arms every week
like goldenrod.

Worse,
the Cling-on's unemployed
and probably unemployable;
you, you're enterprising
and support the whole world
banking community on a crewman's wage.

He boasts and bitches constantly
while you listen with all the intensity
of Captain Kirk.

Why?

It is one of those wonders of the universe.
The Cling-on repents and looks skyward now.
His tears have human salt in them
as he beholds the aurora borealis for the first time.
A better show; this world
is full of wonders, isn't it?
Like you.
A proposal:
Captain, will you marry me?

12/9/86

We now look forward with familiar anticipation
to your nutty serenade from the courtyard
below
announcing your arrival
with those freezer-burned treats
in those shopping bags
you carry with you everywhere
while searching for Mr. Goodgaybar.
Because our brunches have now become
the best part of our weekends, Ed.
Having you here, our marriage has become a family.

But someday you are going to find him, you know,
and probably at the corner of Christopher and Gay
while winning him over with that joint
dangling saucily between your lips.
He'll even know the difference
between founder and flounder.
He'll have *flounder* in *his* shopping bags
and a master's degree
in baking snickerdoodles just like you.
And you'll say to him, "Marry me, my love,
and then let's head up to Brian's and Tom's
for brunch. My treat."
Tra-la-la-dee-da.

But, Ed, come that day
we will miss your pas de un,
done masterfully and reefer-induced
while balancing a glass of Boucheron

in one hand
in our living room
after the serenade arrival.
Because then it will become a pas de deux
done differently
and in the dark
in another room
out in Hoboken.

It's crazy,
but what if he says yes
to the wedding,
but no to the brunch
invitation?

1/31/87

THE BIRTHDAY POEM

You used to think it would end
in another week or two,
but that was three years ago
and now you're twenty-nine
and we're doing just fine.
Happy Birthday.

In your present
I wrap apologies for all future fights
and past ones, for that matter,
and a prayer for your continued success
on the job and so much love
I'll run out of wrapping paper
and I'd even throw in a Volvo stationwagon, too,
if I could afford it.

Someday, you know,
you will call me
when you're in trouble
and in Baghdad, let's say.
Have I ever told you
how far I'd go
just to prove this love?
In this case,
I would come to your rescue
with an Israeli commando squad in tow
and arrive with a band of Dorothy's boys, too,
brandishing omelette pans probably,
but bazookas as well.
Can't you just see us?

Together we'd snatch you
from the tower
from which the infidels
call the faithful to prayer.
And those boys in their Karl Lagerfeld dresses
and Coco Chanel turbins
wouldn't know what hit 'em.

And with the final fight behind us,
you would know
that I love you even more than that,
because I'd also bring to Iraq
one more present I actually give you today
and one which you must never give back:
this heart, in a jewel sack
by Cartier,
with a note: "To my love
born, brilliantly, on Valentine's Day."
Happy Birthday.

2/14/87

The Seduction on Dying Day

(Or, Foot Fetish)

Miss Willoughby
at the clothing store
knows her stuff about men's inches.
How she bears up,
the boss compliments her,
her face all day stuck in the crotches
of little boys without first names,
carrying only mom's MasterCard
or her Visa
to the land of polyester possibilities
and the big wool harvest.

Inseams are her insider's business.
Tucking a testicle
to one side with her left hand,
she stretches the tape
down
to
the
ankle
with the other.
Chatterless.
Next she grips you by the toes
of a warm cotton sock.
"Size nine, boss!" she hollers,
hiding her glee.
"The neck was 13."
Then out comes the overstuffed man

with a businessman's uniform
fated to look silly on a boy of 14.
Miss Willoughby wears a smile.
She knows your secret inches, too.
She is Doctor Willoughby
suddenly
giving you a physical.

How do we bear it,
letting strangers
explore the untouched
pockets of our bodies
when we are boys
being fitted for a funeral suit?
Miss Willoughby is our first defiler,
not Sally after the State game
sophomore year at college
or Denise
on the golf course lawn
after the country club prom.

Women know what they're getting into.
That's why Miss Willoughby smiles
around the ankles
and Denise suggests the fourth fareway
after the dance.
Collectively, women share a sworn secret
learned at summer camp, a pajama party
or a private girls' school somewhere.
There's a formula to be applied to the male anatomy,
unknown even to faggots.
A man's shoe size tells all.
After that,
all inches follow
suit.   1/21/86

It's the damnedest thing, faith defrocked:
so much wound up in a winding sheet.
Quick, someone, a bandage
for the pilgrim's bloodied foot. Save
for him and the Pilgrim
Pope in Rome, am I the only one in the world
tonight worried about the Shroud of Turin?
Frauds are fine
if you've invited them to lighten up
your dinner party, but damn
them if they debunk your dream
of heaven. The news just came
over the car radio: the Shroud,
it said, might as well
be the Tibetan flag
or a dishrag.

Jesus, we believed it touched Your skin.
Once I would have begged the mayor
of Turin to let me touch it, too.
Tonight, John Paul Two,
let us mourn: Muslims somewhere
are having a party
with no liquor
and lots of hashish and jokes about Nazareth.

So, Saviour,
what happens now?
Our faith in shreds,
must we remember to use Gortex

the next time You come?
Meantime, please,
let me borrow Your cave
where I'll sleep it off
this fear I fear
that come morning, and heeding
this latest news, a monk
hiding up in suburban Connecticut,
who is saving the world with his chants,
will let fall his robe, his sorry
head bowed, and sally forth
on a crusade
to resurrect
vaudeville.

                                        10/5/88

OPEN THE DOOR

(AN ANTHEM)

Open the door
God
Here on these steps
to an elusive Heaven
Your altar boys
are now grown up
and, felled by the Love Disease,
have come home
to die.

(Inside
the church, a priest holds up
the skeleton
key and snickers to the pretty nun:
"Silly boys. If only they'd give up
loving *each other*, we'd let them in!")

Inside
where we could lie finally
under Your golden altar, God,
and sing the Requiem with You.
It is not this disease we blame You for,
only the door
closed
to souls
swelled with faith, anger, fear and pain
and needing the sanctuary of Your love.

Open the door
God
Surely You remember
what Death was like,
the seering flesh,
Your cry to Heaven:
Why have You forsaken us?

(EPILOGUE)

and let the boy drop
and fall to Hell

leaving behind a bewildered Christian mom
to lay down the lawn blanket
and plant
his cross

5/1/89

You, once the Law Giver
and Regent by day,
who ruled by right of menu
and hairbrush and Pontiac,
were really just a Margaret so Good
I know
you would have freed the serfs if you could.
But in the end they freed themselves, didn't they?
Now I have found you in the palace
reduced
to a chambermaid.

Once you governed a province
of pediatricians, teachers
and encyclopedia salesmen;
your nod commenced
our footrace to the Christmas tree.
In those days we sought your favor
with crude valentines and a fight
over the hedgeclippers.
Today your domain has finally shrunken
to a washing machine
and seven evergreens that comprise
the palace guard out front,
which you trim tenderly
and ever so slower each year.

Mom, I have come home
and now the suspenseful walk
down the lengthening hallway

past the bogeyman furnace,
once your walk,
finds you napping as serenely
as a Mother Goose princess.
I am sorry.
I learned too late
the sad storybook tale
of your own childhood in a tyrant's land
and the doubletime you did
later in yet another kingdom
to pay the pediatrician's taxes in ours.
Palace scuttlebutt has it
that twice you even carried
the royal dead inside you
cheerfully, like a state secret,
and gave them names, lute-sounding,
that they would never hear.

As I stand over you
the king is holding court in the living room,
berating a TV set.
He stills calls you Queeny sometimes.
Here in this little room,
mother, I finally bring you terms of surrender.
But the battle is done, isn't it?
And this puppy lying beside you
guards your warm side now
usurping my rightful place
when I was your Prince of Wails.
But, mother ...
mother, may I
move him closer, touch a regal brow,
return the bedtime kiss?

2/2/87

A Republican, Taking a Stroll,
    Encounters God on a Beach

(For my Father)

It was in autumn, 1974,
when they met accidentally
along God's glorious
creation of a seascape.

At last,
thought the man,
I will learn
the answers
to all the Great Questions.

"Tell me, God," he spoke,
"did Honest Abe ever
make it into Heaven
despite his criminal
disregard of the U.S.
Constitution? And
does Hoover forever
have to take the rap
for his predecessor's
Depression?"

God smiled and tossed
a Rock of Ages out to sea,
but did not answer.

"Our Roosevelt

suffered from the sin
of pride, I know,"
said the man, "but
he was really
just a Teddy bear."

There was a burp
from the upset waves beyond
and a seagull let go
a death squeal
as the man waited for God
to reply, but the Grand Old One
just stood there,
looking like a statue
of Himself,
or Chester A. Arthur.

The man talked on:
"It was Harding who
brought back normalcy
and Taft who bust the trusts up.
Calvin may have been
too cool to calm
the maelstrom of his times,
but the Grand Old Party
did emancipate the slaves
and President Grant assured
their voting rights. We even
turned the other cheek
and forgave the Red Chinese
their heresy."

Silently then, God looked
away, reached into the surf
and pulled a fish out.

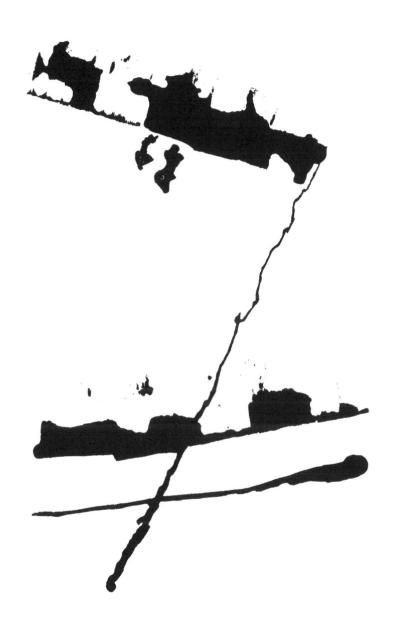

He thought of multiplying
it for fun,
but threw it back.

"The Democrats
did the Devil's bidding
and started all the wars,"
the man added. "We Republicans
brought peace. Talk to me —
please! — and tell me, God,
am I forgiven?"

The man dropped to his knees
as if to invite a salty baptism
and begged the Other's
Pardon.

But instead of speaking,
even softly, God took out
a big stick and drew —
it was a donkey — in the sand,
and the man cried out:
"No! Not you ... you, too?!"

God smiled and was about to walk on,
out over the water, in fact,
but hesitated.
Finally, He spoke.
Turning to
Nixon, He winked,
and whispered privately:
"Yes, My son.
But I, too, liked Ike."

1/16/87

A Selfish Raging
Against Your Church in Rome

First of all, it preaches
that man is basically Evil
(read Original Sin).
Blasphemy?! Next, ya learn
ya can't even kill yourself:
to a mere mortal,
it's a mortal sin.
(Christ, You could do it.
Or does Rome still say we blame the Jews for You?)

Since You left
it's technically become
the world's largest corporation
You'll be glad to know,
cranking out assembly-line Catholics
faster than General Motors
can make defective cars.
Should the poor resist
by slipping on a condom in the dark, however,
they risk getting the backside
of a ruby-studded hand.
The Pope waves his
from a palace balcony.

Your priests aren't married
because too many of them
got syphillis in another century.
A lot of them don't care, though,
because they're gay anyway.

Oh, this isn't another old crying out
against the Inquisition or the selling
of an indulgence here or there.
We're now discussing the classroom sadism
of Little Sisters in Your name.

The Pope says he's infallible.
I realize even You've made Your mistakes,
but have You had a chat with him
since 1870?

Off to Gehenna one of these days, God.
There's a old saint, dying
of loneliness, up in Buffalo
about to masturbate
and blow
the whole thing.
He'll be joining me.

                                        1/30/87

So You Cry Heresy, Hetero

You're taking this too seriously.
You must know
that it was Gift from Him
like a clarion voice,
being amber-eyed or double-jointed.
I had as much say
in the matter as deciding
I'd be black or white,
left-handed or a Muslim,
for that matter.

But, oh, I do love thy Lord
and we are bitchy to each other
because He set the rules
and the game is rough.
I once wanted so desperately
out of it and the inside
scoop on the N.F.L. game
and just back into a woman's womb.
Just think how mom and dad would admire
Eve, my blonde wife, peeling
apples on our back porch.
But blame Someone Else for the bad call,
not me,
and leave me
to the one
I have taken as a wife.
We love each other
so seriously
and play no games

without announcing
the rules ahead of time
and even pray sometimes
before we score.
Come Judgment Day,
He will decide the score.

2/1/87

God stood on the corner
of Broadway and 42nd Street
and told the little children
to suffer unto Him one mo' time.
With needle holes between
their toes and chancres
on their fannies, they cried,
"Hell, no! God damn!
We've suffered long enough!
If it's finally all over with,
we're heading to the discos
downtown!"

There was ice cream, free,
for everyone while it lasted;
movie houses showed the very,
very last picture show
and murderers suddenly
found their jobs obsolete.

Phone lines buzzed
with "I'm sorry, dad"; a robed
man in Rome finally passed out rubies
to cripples under a rotunda;
then there was the story
of the reluctant virgin
in Salt Lake City who tried
to commit a last, quick rape,
but found his plumbing wouldn't work;
and no graves stirred.

A desert bloomed
with pomegranates
in Ethiopia and somebody pressed
The Button
and nothing happened.

When a confused Buddhist monk
in Japan heard the news
that the Christian Finale
was at hand, he tried
to commit hari-kari,
but his sword turned into
a lily-of-the-field.

Wine was turned back into water
everywhere, and vodka
was changed into potato soup,
but even the Russians
didn't seem to mind.

Meanwhile, carefree bankers
burned all the world's money
in one magnificent bonfire
at the corner of Wall
and Broad streets.

Then
the Holy Family
appeared on the horizon,
took a bow,
and the world in unison
exclaimed, "Why?"
But Jesus just smiled
and reached up and turned
the sun off,

a garden snake crawled back
into his hole in New Jersey,
God-the-Father sent everybody home,
and Mary, His wife, sent everybody
thank-you notes.

1/16/87

— Amen —

P.S.

A post script
to the reader:
you can't have
sex with God,
dummy,
because His boyfriend,
John the Baptist,
wouldn't permit it;
neither would Mrs. Christ,
née Magdalene,
who has enough problems.

1/30/87

P.P.S.

Sorry, Savior,
for that last little joke.
We've both been rather rough
on each other.
But here's a proposition:
You give me and Brian
our own begotten son
and You can be our centerfold
Man of the Year.

I had a sacrilegious
dream the other night
that You fed us
the Holy Eucharist under
a sun-filled dome
while the Holy See
watched on,
horrified,
but suddenly saw the light.

It will be on that day, Redeemer,
that You finally throw open the closet doors
like prison gates along Castro Street
and Your monks will step out,
squinting at the Son,
their chains dropping off them
like dirty condoms onto the stones.

Together then
we will all swim

babybutt naked
through that shining eye
to redemption's shore;

and Brian and I will be holding up
our newborn son — glorious,
Godlike — into that light
for Your kiss.

1/30/87

Romans 1:27

And men gave
up
natural intercourse
with women and were consumed
with lust for one another.
Men
did shameful
acts with men,
and thus received
in themselves
the penalty for their perversity.

57 A.D.

BOOK II

THE ASHES OF EDEN

"Let my lusts be my ruin then,
since all else is a fake and a mockery."

— Hart Crane

GRANT'S TOMB

Pssst, Ulysses.
It's dark out here
and Tom out here
(from the neighborhood)
parked on your steps
in my field jacket this winter night
saying out loud, sir, crying out loud:
I hereby grant
you and this world
Unconditional Surrender.

News came this day
from the front: my BlackLove
of Lee's Virginia, sir,
tests positive
for the Big A invasion.
There's one more battle in the field tonight.
May we raise the sword together?

High
on
your
dark step
this hour I see with the eyes
of your spreadeagle sentries:
there, south, Brian's blood spills off
a Greenwich Village pier
and flows out to a poisoned sea.
Help me. I have never cried like this
nor known such love or fear of battle.

Send for reinforcements, sir.
We are dying, hero,
dying.

I did not choose him
lightly, sir, by the way.
There was no sale at the Valentine shop
the day I bought the black card, my envelope.
We met in your neighborhood
on a night I drank as you once did
when I encountered someone shopping, too,
and so happy to have found
a clearance sale.
I surrendered on the spot
and he took me home from the bar
where once you would have stayed all night
and played the old songs
on an even older quarter.
But Brian was my truest conqueror.
Six years he once served in your Union Marines
and like Helen
is now worth fighting for.

Or like your Julia.

Pssst, Ulysses.
I have a little joke for ya.
Who, they ask, is buried in Grant's Tomb?
We are.
Behind me are your bones
black from the cancer that finally felled you
and I am with you on this wintry night
when Julia leans to the right
and whispers to your corpse
the pillowwords I sadly overhear:

"We lie here, love,
at last
in state
together."

Someday, too,
Brian and I, you know, will share
the Immortal Room.

President Grant,
friend, union saviour,
we have been neighbors now for five years counting,
the corpses are mounting,
the call is made:
Rise, Ulysses, commander-in-chief!
You are needed this time
in another century.

Past midnight now;
boys walk by
and poke through the park trees
looking for sex.
In at least one
of them a bomb ticks
hidden in his loins. Once
I might have sprung up
and walked beside him,
winking at love.
But this is not the same game now,
but war,
though the walking dead
seem not to care, or you
who yet refuses
to rise
even as this next day threatens to.

I put one foot up
then another
while waiting for the light
or you to catch me.
I am dancing, U.S.,
dancing on our grave, I guess.
"Let Us Have Peace."

1/26/89

My own test results are miraculous:
HIV negative.

But midnight reprieves are always ominous:
What kind of life could it be
in a world without B?

And I wonder: Does this mean that someday
I could end up being The Last Man on Earth
Adam at the end of his rope
his sexual exile
from Eden
who turns out to be gay?
Almighty Genesis God
might suddenly have to come down
with a severe case
of a sense of humor

1/89

Who else would you have found
to love you as I do?
One boy may have been more muscled,
taller, too, a real looker sweeping down Broadway,
but Ian, let's call him, would have promised more
yet the casbah is crowded
and boxes from Tiffany's you've opened before.
The point is: amour. And I have loved you
with a frenzied heart, you know,
and one eye open at night
searching for God.

As I watch for the night sweats, too.
This disease makes you bleed your own juices,
although tonight I see cool dreams
sweep over you like meadow winds.
We will be fine for one more day.
Forgive me this nightwatch, please, Brian.
You'd be angered to know I'm mothering
and furious over these fantasies of Ian in your arms
but it's his fatal seed that you sweat
in the dark; and I am still truly proud
of how hard I work at this love
and of winning you

1/10/89

With the old camera left behind
on some vacation backstreet, the new one comes
this day by UPS, welcomed
like an emergency, last-minute Boswell
who gave up writing so he could become more flashy.

Or is he that cocky reporter, I wonder, come to profile us
before the hangman knocks? We do not care,
but juggle the black box hurriedly
as we pose for playful, self-timed shots
to be shared later on only with a bewildered processor
at the Fotomat who must wonder
at our grinning insistence on life,
two men hand in hand, black and white
on color film: frozen moments in a private
danse macabre
he was not invited to

To catch the smile before it fades
the body upright, temporarily triumphant,
framed in a picture that must be taken
now now now

Inside the box
the film clicks forward so fast
it's like a motion picture almost
of two Pocono nightclub performers, say,
who fell in love and hammed it up
up in their private cabin once the club closed.
One of them would kid, though,

as they took those shots of each other:
"Bang, bang
I shoot you dead
ha! ha!" because
comics are never funny

Some years later I will finger these prints
with an old love and a future knowing
but that night, my love,
were were *Gentleman's Quarterly*
models, remember? — no, movie stars!
— or let's just face it: two men hungry
for life, frightened between the cheeses,
because there was no way we could know
that next afternoon when we sent the film in
what would develop

4/19/89

KEY WEST

(OR, REREADING HEMINGWAY)

Papa knew best even then
before all the gays got here
dragging their furry boas from that northern clime
so they could don them along with the parrot's plume
and dance *grande* till dawn.
Now hear the bells, drums
and boom-boom, local butchboys.
This gay-la can go on forever.
One distant night ago
when you still ruled
our mutual Papa
tore up the timber bar at Captain Tony's
and carried a urinal home,
he-man-style, for fun.
All these fags
today get pissed
on pina coladas
and carry only
MasterCard

and, *si*, their heads
higher, too,
for this place.

Faggots
going down on America
finally found their haven
this far south

in the last resort.

But what do all you butchboys think?
Take heed from Papa.
Here's for whom the bell
really tolled then — and now:
quote, *All the best ones,*
when you thought it over, were gay.
It was much better to be gay
and it was a sign of something, too ...
like having immortality
*while you were still alive.**

*From *For Whom the Bell Tolls*, written in Key West, late 1930s.

117

GOD TOURS THE BATTLEFIELD

Wincing as He performed His Last Judgment duties,
God tiptoed between the fallen bodies
like a disgusted nun at an orgy.
Ooo, there's a naked one! He shrieked,
the Almighty Plague Dog,
then snapped His fingers
to transform Himself into Bozo,
a disguise He decided might amuse
(read confuse) the wounded.

Seeing a bloodied one stir,
He stooped to listen, careful
to hold back His Breath of Life.
Was it a corny old rock 'n' roll lyric
the boy quoted, causing God
to howl so and run off? No.
Just imagine the nerve telling Bozo:
Life is a passing carnival show,
all blue smoke, whistles and bells
it doesn't mean a goddamn thing
and it's gone tomorrow

1/23/91

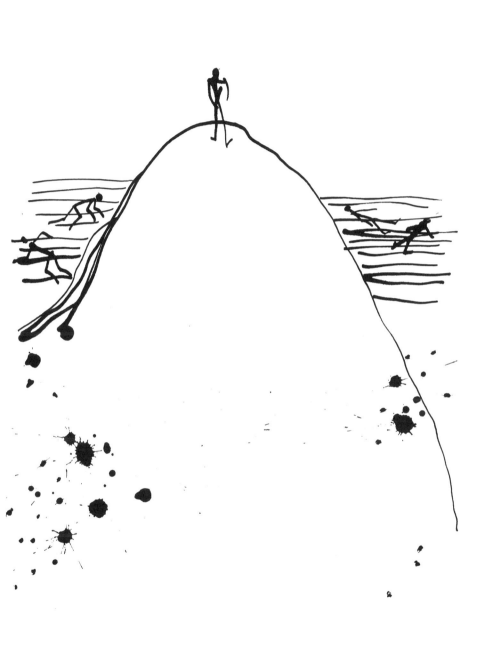

If Steven and Mark don't matter now
(shortly after they were married
at a tea dance at Russian River, remember,
Steven ran off with that twinkie from Seattle,
Mark moved to New Hope
and we never heard from either of them again)
why should I care
about making any new friends today? Tell me.
The old ones are just dying off
or else, spooked by the plague,
are running off
the edge of the world.
All I can remember of Steven and Mark now is singing
"We'll
all
go
down
together!"
with them and Billy Joel
that night of the blue daiquiris.

The hardest thing about this life
is looking through an old address book
and trying not to peek through the "X"s
because corpses sometimes peek back
through those inky crosses
I finally made
a year after we buried them.

Who won the World Series last year?

I can't remember
and don't want to, come to think of it.
Knowing would be like remembering
that old job where I once worked so hard,
was never promoted, and where no one
would remember me today.
Some things just don't matter
and the worst part about it
is that you never know which ones they are at the time.

Touch, touch my eyes, children of the earth,
and show me a wonderland around the corner
where you can eat the wildflowers
where giants dance
and the old songs play forever

1/30/91

A SMALL VICTORY AT BRIANSBURG

Pssst, Ulysses.
I have a little news for ya:
we are still trooping   along.

9/29/89

MAUI

Fleeing west to catch a setting sun
we land in paradise
where God once called these lava isles
up from an empty sea
and lasooed the sun,
so folklore says, to keep them warm
for the minah and today two boys at play.
There are silver pools and fountains
of forever
everywhere
we look; we drink

Words with *iao*, *uau*
sound painful to say
but as long as we stay
blissfully far away
from Mr. and Mrs. Detroit at the luau
we are free
at last to lei under the monkeypod trees
and rediscover ourselves
and the world as it must have felt at creation's dawn.
I am browning like you, my love.
I swim now through this mai tai
to your private shore
and bite the red hibiscus
smiling
eat me

9/28/89

125

LETTER TO TOMMY

What would you have looked like,
I often wonder — boy of this black Irishman
and his black (nay, almond) lover?
As if you are here I say: Sit up, Tommy.
Drink the last of your milkshake. And listen.
I have our story to tell.

It was a dark casino island I came to win in 1979.
Your mother, too.
On the night we met, we took each other's hand,
surveyed the town with exhilarating fear,
and asked: But what will we do when the game is over?
Looking heavenward, your mother said:
Someday
I want to die
into that midnight.
Sky.

Then we won the city in a crap game
rigged actually so that someone else should have won it
and we scrambled off with our winnings
and took them to our bed.
Your mother felt his first night sweat that evening
as we clung to each other like children spooked.
You were conceived at 11:59 p.m., Tommy,
at which alarming time
our coins all spilled off the sheets
and crashed to the floor.

Each morning after that I awoke with wonder:

Would Lazarus be rising or falling today?
But then your mother would rise
brilliantly with the eastern light
and make his way to the shower, nibbling on almonds,
as I would marvel again at the glory of resurrections.
Morninglow back then
gave him the outline
as he retreated
of a naked black angel.

Dear Tommy,
if only you could know
our perfect Manhattan faggot household
filled with Krups coffee grinders, gourmet pizza pans
and Waldo, our stuffed St. Bernard, who waits
at the front door salivating over the promise of your
navy blue pant leg
returning from Sacred Heart Elementary.
On that sunny schoolday afternoon when you'd finally
come home your mother would bake something sweet
and dark and chewy for you to munch on
and typical of the Species Yuppie,
like pumpernickel pizza.

He is a remarkable man, your mother,
you'll be glad to know —
a bronzed Marilyn with brains
who broke the bank at 52nd Street
when he was promoted to vice-president at 32!
Tommy, you never suckled at his tit
as I have because of a cowardly Victorian God
who never showed the world His ankles.
But know this: his breastfood is sweeter
than butterscotch
milkshake, than life.

We had dreams of you winning the Grand Prix someday,
you know, and cultivating the moon's soil
so you could bring forth, miraculously, dandelion wine,
an achievement for which you would
be pictured, slightly schnockered, on the front page
of *The New York Times*, of course.
Our neighbors would all call that morning
with spirited congratulations.

But what must you look like now,
a boy frightened of the dark
sky where you real angels hide?

Tommy, our boy,
did we lose you finally in a shopping mall
when you slipped off to see the clown
at the Yum Yum Yogurt opening
and I turned to look for a drugstore for fever pills?
Or was it amidst the hubbub at the casino
while your parents were busy with the one-armed
banditbosses?
Come home
playtime is over
midnight calls
and your comforter of blue spun sugar
waits
warmed underneath
by the sweat of your mother
who today
(hurry, Tommy,
run run run)
is
about to fall

1/23/91

MR. FIX-IT

Out in the country
you get to know all the folks
like the kindly old couple Jesus is talking to
who own the hardware store: Mr. and Mrs. Turn,
who were married in the church 50 years ago
and lived happily ever after (their son
is a bigshot in the Knights of Columbus).
Jesus needs to buy some tool
with the word "universal" in it,
but Old Man Turn can't find it
and Mrs. Turn is suddenly needed on aisle two.
So, Jesus, I say, striking up a conversation,
I'm in a rush, but don't worry.
You've got a bigger job to do.
Tell me: how many faggots went to Hell today?

Jesus bolts away from me
to find Old Man Turn
who is lost among the monkey wrenches
and 2-inch screws
while I follow along, curious
as to what it is they're looking for.

Finally, exasperated,
I ask the Old Man to help me please,
but he is lost in wonderment at not being able
to resolve his "universal" quest
while looking straight into the eye of God.
Please, sir, I say, *my house is burning,*
the roof is off the top and I need to buy the store.

129

Hearing me, he just throws his arms up,
hands me the keys and ushers his wife
out the front door.
Then Jesus turns to me
with a kindly voice
and asks for help

7/93

UNDER SIEGE

It's useless. We're surrounded.
AIDS has now ensnared its most unbelievable victim:
the dutiful volunteer behind every charity,
that sweet-grinned champion baker of molasses
cookies, my Brian.
Walled up in a fortress of medical armaments,
we are trapped, Brian is bedridden,
and the enemy is within.

There's no point in becoming the furious papa
("This will not go on in my house!")
or St. Joan surrendering to the fire starter.
Our plan is simple.
Suddenly believing in miracles,
we lie in wait, two old Floridians,
Irving and Sylvia, bitter at life
but glad to have each other,
who never step out in the sun.

Since this disease is a matter of stiff bones
and lying around on afternoons
we relive our eight years together again
out loud,
pebble by pebble,
like topaz stones in our hands
claimed along the way in our grand crusade.

"I guess I'll never go back to work again,"
he tells a friend one day
who must wonder at his tears

and mine suddenly, too, remembering
it's time for our yearly Caribbean trip.
("Oh, which island should we try out *next*?!"
we used to gush with wonder each fall.)
But our friends and his family back us up bravely
as we suffer the invasion of syringes,
tubes, iodine pads, plastic gloves,
diapers, a walker, and a tabletop forest
of pill bottles that must,
just judging from the sheer number of them,
somewhere inside hold The Cure.
Three times a day Brian makes a meal of them:
red (are they sweet?), green (bitter?)
and shiny white (oh, please let these hold
the luminous promise behind winter skies)

Before he popped the vaults of Wall Street,
Brian was an aspiring actor
doing Brecht in the deli checkout line
and singing "Corner of the Sky" at Broadway auditions.
Here beside his fallen form now, I am writing books
about winners
of Emmy and Grammy Awards.

His pleasures are small:
He discovers iced Hawaiian punch to go with his chips
while warming himself in the glow
of old Hollywood chestnuts flickering
on the fire inside a TV set.
Myrna Loy pulls a fruitcake out one day
and, smiling, invites him to try it.
Freddie Bartholomew eggs him on
to come out and build a snowboy.

Trying to cuddle with him at night,

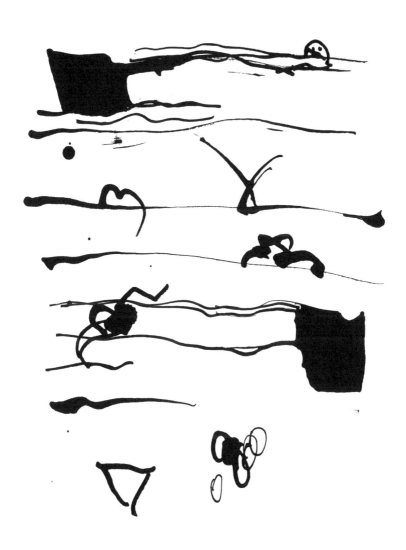

I am overwhelmed with how not to squish
him like the potato chip bag.
But then he rocks himself into a new position
and announces, "Ready. OK now. Try it again."
I want to surrender to dreamy sleep in his arms,
remembering when we were Frankie and Johnny
once lusting across these sheets, but I am careful
of the new vein sprouting from his chest
up
Heavenward
where a bag hangs
labeled "Life. Poison."

But at least I am holding on
and he is, too, with fingers cupped behind my neck.
I'm here, baby, I say. *The arguments never happened,*
I love you, too,
and I will make sure you die an easy death.
But hold on for now and close your eyes ...
Instantly, we are back on St. Bart's
lying on a beach of razor shells
laughing
and then sipping cappuccino
in a Barbados cafe
waiting for a storm to pass.

It's at night that the fight becomes the hardest
when we are ambushed by fever chills
("More blankets! More!" he cries as I pile them on)
and vomiting bouts that produce
chunks of his soul in our hands.
There are separate buckets beside his side of the bed:
1.) for vomit
2.) for pee.
I empty them constantly ...

as he lies there wearing
the unflappable grandfather's smile,
which tells me he's still OK.
Saints are made of this, I think.
But why, oh, why, doesn't he just once
raise a fist to the Furies and shout:
"I do not deserve this!
I am a martyr to love!"

Sometimes we stay up
the rest of the night,
two girls at a pajama party bearing their souls at 3 a.m.
Did you ever have an affair with Rudy? I inquire.
He scoffs the question off.
Where do you think you got AIDS? I finally ask.
He tells me in two words
and I nod in understanding.
Are you angry that I'm not sick, too?
Tell me the truth. I've got to know.
He reaches out and convinces me
with a wild embrace
that my fate is his only joy left.

These are some of the wonderful things
about taking the long bow.
The needles and diapers
are almost worth it
if it means that lovers, caught up
in a real life and death drama
they know will end tragically, can still take the stage
and know the heightened passions of love as art.
Brewing up hot chocolate for Brian in the kitchen,
even wiping down his dirty bum
or dozing on his shoulder in the afternoon,
I know perfect love.

Dying is the ultimate intimacy of marriage,
we learn, and discover, too, that you get to say
everything to each other
that never gets said
like
I surrender
I am sorry
and
goodbye

It was the vertical city that let them go
killing them.
Andy couldn't keep his skirts down
here and so the Love Bug got up under them
and bit the prick finally.
Crazy Ed sucked the crack candy too hard
and threw himself in front of that train:
the image is a *film noir* frame
forever frozen in my mind.
Then the Love Bug found my lover
after it took us so many years to find each other.
Tonight
he
is
falling

I have thrown the net out, lover,
and sounded the call.
The same family you once wondered might run
the other way once you got sick
are running here, in planes and cars,
just as they've rallied each time you've needed them
ever since you broke the news.
Hold on. Mama will soon be at your bedside again
like she was when you first screamed
upon waking up to life. Your brothers
are bringing their Spalding catcher's mitts.

Watching you fall
brings on a thrilling terror.

The drama proves that movies and books can be real.
This must be happening to George Brent
or Icarus, I think, as the film
slips into a dark dream scene
that takes place near a swamp beyond New York.
Suddenly, you
          flutter
down
                          in
                                                    a
          winding   path
 like a
                blackbird
                felled
by homo-hating sportsmen
who click their elephant guns together
overhead in triumph after they nail you
and dare me to draw near

What does it feel like
to dive the Great Hole?
You must wonder if you'll hit water soon
and resurface in a paradise archipelago.
Or does it feel like
being drawn into the great Holy Hand
or like the soapy wineglass —
or the wiggling infant —
dropped?

I cannot catch you, sweetheart.
Your velocity is too great
and you are too busy going someplace
I cannot follow.
"Am I dying?" you asked just hours ago.
"Yes. Are you afraid?" my voice shook.

You turned your head silently to the wall
as I fled
and ran for hours, it seemed,
one more lunatic raging
through mad city streets
looking for God.
Once I got home I reached your mother on the phone:
Hurry, I said. *Somebody has dropped the baby ...*

4/4/92

It is now months later
and all is just as dizzying.
When you see Andy in the underworld
would you tell him I forgive him
for stealing my MasterCard?
And then find Ed and slap him for me, saying:
How dare you throw your life away
while we fought so hard to save this one?
How can it be
that in just one year
I lost my whole gay family?

But at least I officially became part of yours in the siege,
our arms ever interlocked in the fumbling grasp
to pull you up.
Together we will always be platoon veterans
who survived the war
but not the memory of the massacre
of the innocent

And at least they got to your bedside in time.
But I will never know how your mama knew
exactly
the moment you would slip away,

140

the same uncanny way mothers
know the weather will change
even before the temperature falls.
It was three a.m. in your hospice room.
Quietly, she roused me,
your brothers and sisters nearby
and had us join her at your bedside
where we watched thunderstruck —

You made a ghoulish face
and let go

Your last words, demented,
were that you were off to see a play that night
and you were driving

Between us I hold the record
for having the longest fall.
Years it took before you finally stopped me
from diving into that liquor bottle
one more time
where I had planned to reach the underworld
before you, weave asbestos blankets
(would you need them?)
and find Andy and Ed
so we could knit our unholy fingers together,
just inches above the fiery tongues of devils,
catch you,
and be together again

But now the horror movie is back on the mind's screen
with an orchestra playing
the only music that could ever properly underscore,
in the made-for-TV Story of Our Lives,
the terror I felt when I first had the thought —

oh, thief of sleep and arsonist of souls —
that is the most horrible thing about all of this:
You saved my life.
But when it came my turn to save yours
I won 5,000 medals trying
but I lost
and
let
you
down

1/17/93

V-G DAY

Pssst, Ulysses.
We lost the uncivil war, I guess.

Because there are no gays in the U.S. military,
we will go find a separate tomb.

But, meantime, sir, excuse me.
There's a dispatch from the Enemy
to our commander-in-chief:

God waits
at Appomattox,
wearing a party hat

11/12/93

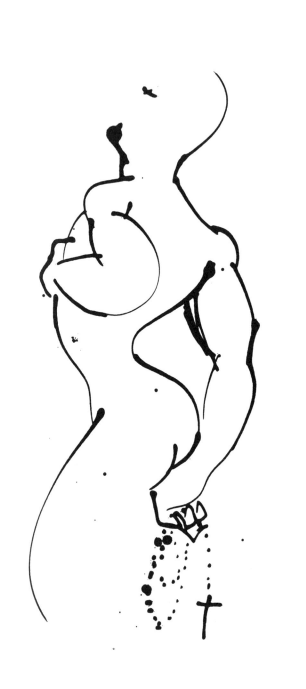

JUDGMENT DAY

Spying the urn
across the room at dusk,
I wonder: In a world of such dragons,
why do I stalk the church?
Is it because it stalks "Satyrs at Play,"
a bas relief on the bolted doors of St. Peter's
that recalls a time when the satyrs' stiff pricks
pointed heavenward?
Or because Cardinal Spellman once swished
at those drag queen fêtes at the Plaza Hotel
with J. Edgar Hoover
then, back at the cathedral,
slapped his limp wrists at fairies
who craved the Body of Christ?

And does it matter?
Will the Catholic Jesus, dressed
in a radiant Christian Dior gold gown,
really meet me on Judgment Day
when I am finally ravished from AIDS
and say, "It's OK, kid. Actually, I'm proud of ya.
At least you didn't commit one mortal sin —
at least you didn't wear a condom."

Letter to Heaven:
Keeping the faith
is hard in a ruined Eden
where the list of hardships
begins so
with "A."   3/6/93

145

After the greatest defeat,
what's another?

Hi, mom and dad.
Guess what.
I'm a faggot
you had a son-in-law
he was black
a Protestant
and he just died
of AIDS.

For a lifetime I have imagined the day
I would finally unfurl
my fairy wings before the two of them:
I had expected to be lifted up
in the air from the hot blast that would follow next,
up to a planet lost in childhood skies
(where, yes, boys do mate with boys; it's a gay life
on my native world Nocturn).
But they are sitting there, not fluttering,
mom and dad — it's unbelievable —
like bombardment victims so still and silent
I am tempted to revive them with Holy Water.
No priest would do it, after all,
and thereby grant them a house call
ever since mom burnt that meatloaf
we served the new parish priest back in 1972.

Once I assured them I was HIV-negative and flew

back to New York, they phoned to talk about it all.
Ma Bell was calling the candidate
to say, at this late hour,
he finally took the state of Ohio.
Brian once would have screamed hallelujah at the news,
but today I am shellshocked by it
and overcome by a new mystery of this world:
They really mean it
when they say
they love me still
and wish they had known my lover.
Oh, dear gray heads, beloved forebears,
you have just lifted yourselves up
to a pantheon
where I hope, I pray
you live forever

10/28/93

WATERLOO

The world did not conspire to ruin
the moment for us, you'll be glad to know —
this morning at the lake in Pennsylvania
when I walked, scared and sobbing
like an orphan lost in these woods,
to the place "you know,
where we used to skip stones."
There at the shoreline we would make our last goodbye,
you once decided, before I'd surrender your ashes
to the bully world
that once conspired to drown us
in fever sweat, vomit
and margaritas

The fish around the dock
jumped and scattered, you know,
as I dropped your ashes in puffs above their heads
like a benediction of cumulus clouds.
Ashes to aqua, dust to dark water
you went
down
swirling in the unseen current
into the shape of an eagle one moment
— then a blackbird, before the clouds vanished
into specks of gray that rained onto the stones
and sunken driftwood below

In these waters of life
you are home again.

Goodbye.
A child inside me died today, Brian,
after he smashed all his storybooks
with their fairytale endings
against the rocks along this shore
and dove into the water
to lay down beside you forever.
Life is too grotesque at this moment
to appreciate the glories of nature here
at your graveside — the black trees frozen
in their reach to heaven,
the lulling water that blankets you now
(and I am grateful for it)
as I perform our funereal rite on this late day in spring.
We never bought that canoe we always said
we would for this lake, you know. Why
do I think of that now?

Because today I am a Navy wife
left standing at the pier during wartime.
She glances out at the gray ship pulling away
that will never bring back her life's cargo alive,
and she knows it,
but still goes back to their cabin
with a heart full of hope
and makes soup for two

5/6/92

149

THE HAUNTING

(OR, THE LAST DANCE)

It's been nine months since you died
and I should be giving birth to a new life
so why am I still rearranging the pictures
in the photo albums trying to make the story
come out with a happy ending?
And why do I keep the torn jeans
and your "Just Visiting This Planet" T-shirt
in the bottom drawer and begin each day
with a waltz with your ghost
(Jesus, step aside!)
asking him, "Remember that scary helicopter ride
when we almost plunged into the volcano?"

Dating is hard
because it means I must surrender your spot
under the electric blanket
where you'd once call out to me as I was en route
to the john during a break
in *Star Trek: The Next Generation*: "Two scoops
of vanilla and don't forget to zap it a little
in the microwave!"
Even dead, you are a lingering presence I can't evict.
Faced with the prospect of a new lover
who prefers *Benny Hill* reruns
and granola bars,
I prefer a ghostly monster
representing the Great Galactic Mystery
and the cold sweet stuff

I do go out to the bars in New York
and bring boys home,
but then something always goes wrong.
There's a shriek in the dark
when I realize it's Marcus or Jerry there
and he wonders if he's suddenly hurt me
with a playful bite.

Christmas just passed.
It was the first time in years
I didn't put up a tree.
By the way, honey, I have discovered 2 percent milk
and the cement patchup job I gave the chimney
out at the cabin didn't hold, just like you said.
That's all the news ... and — oh! — those books
on TV and music I was working on before you died
have now hit print
and I'm on TV, too.

"Do you ever think about the irony
that your life is taking off
just as mine is slipping away?"
you once asked me in between
fever bouts one afternoon
after vomiting your pills.
"Constantly," I confessed
and think of it now
again as I grip your ghost harder
and we dip into the graceful swoon
of the waltz's finale.

Don't go.
I am counting on you haunting me
into old age.
I'll be out in the kitchen one future morning

in the country
pouring your favorite mint coffee
for my new lover and me
when I forget the dance for the first time.
You will tap me on the shoulder
and remind me of the milk,
which suddenly, miraculously
becomes whole

1/15/93

Thomas O'Neil's freelance articles have appeared in *The New York Times*, *The Los Angeles Times*, *TV Guide* and other leading publications. His plays include *Judy at the Stonewall Inn,* written for the 25th anniversary celebration of the Stonewall riots in Greenwich Village that launched the gay rights movement. He is also the author of two definitive showbiz award books — *The Grammys: For the Record* and *The Emmys: Star Wars, Showdowns and the Supreme Test of TV's Best* (Penguin Books).

Ty Wilson's passionate style of romantic illustration has earned him the rank as one of America's most popular artists, whose best-selling posters and serigraphs are sold through Bruce McGaw Graphics. His other works include pop album covers, Broadway theater posters, graphics for women's athleticwear and illustrations that have appeared in the pages of *Vogue, Harper's Bazaar* and *Vanity Fair*.

For additional copies of *Sex With God,*
send $6.95 plus $2 for postage and handling to:
Wexford Press, 185 Claremont Ave., Suite 6A,
New York, N.Y. 10027